Protecting

Your Money

From Yourself

Protecting Your Money From Yourself

A Retiree's Guide to Insuring You Have Enough Money to Enjoy Your Retirement

Bryan Sullivan

Published by Vellum Financial, 805 Aerovista Place, Suite 205, San Luis Obispo, CA 93401   Phone (805) 546-1000

Printed in the United States of America

ISBN-13: 978-1463765545
ISBN-10: 1463765541

I dedicate this book to my father who taught me to save (and save early), give to God, live within my means, buy quality and share with others.

About The Author

For more than 19 years, Bryan has been a financial advisor helping individuals and families achieve their financial planning goals, by providing advice on Investment Planning; Insurance Planning; Tax Planning; Retirement Planning; Estate Planning; Intergenerational Wealth Transfer Planning; and Educational Savings Planning. Working with a network of highly skilled professionals in San Luis Obispo, CA he has dedicated his career to providing high-quality advice and integrated wealth management solutions that simplify and enhance the quality of his clients' lives.

Bryan became a licensed financial advisor in 1992 and worked with several Wall Street firms including Merrill Lynch and UBS until creating an independent, SEC-Registered investment advisory firm in 2009 - Vellum Financial.

It is his belief that the RIA platform is the final step in the evolutionary process toward providing unbiased investment management to their clients. In creating Vellum Financial, he has created a strictly objective financial advisory firm that incorporates "best practices" of investment management while avoiding the many negatives of the brokerage industry

Vellum Financial is the embodiment of his uncompromising focus on the client. Bryan aims to provide objective advice, complete transparency and unique access to "best-in-class" subject matter experts.

The firm that he has created gives him the opportunity to shape his own culture and to establish a higher standard of service and performance within his industry. Indeed, Vellum Financial represents an ethical, intellectual and deeply personal opportunity as owner-operator - the opportunity that culminates in allowing them to be a true steward of your assets.

A strong contributor to the community, Bryan has volunteered with the Morro Bay Lions Club and Big Brother Big Sisters organization. Resident in San Luis Obispo since 1994, Bryan and his wife Tricia, and their 4 children share a passion for outdoor activities and spending time with friends and family.

You can schedule a **FREE** Consultation with Bryan now and take the Guided Discovery™ Tour by calling **1-800-546-0123.**

FREE
OFFER!

You Can Schedule A **FREE** Consultation With Bryan Now and Take The Guided Discovery™ Tour By Calling **1-800-546-0123**

Bryan is offering you a **FREE** guide called, "The Critical Questions You Must Ask To Get Your Financial Life In Order"

You can obtain the guide online at:
http://www.VellumFinancial.com/freeguide

Foreword

In reading Bryan Sullivan's book, "Protecting Your Money From Yourself", I can reflect on my own learning curve as this author took the time and effort to apply to my account all of the expertise he speaks of in this manuscript. From our first meeting when I came to him wanting him to make investments of my nest egg in something that would safely grow and not run any risk of loss, he sat me down and explained some of the financial facts of life that are described in this book. He has captured the essence of our relationship as team members in the management of personal financial affairs.

His approach has been to enable all of his clients to make better decisions by pointing out facts that I had never been aware of and teaching a more appropriate approach in the handling of these affairs. On occasion, this involved his holding classes for several of his clients to acquaint us with the meaning of financial terms and how to interpret the language of investing. I see in these pages his continuing efforts to work together with clients and to be their guide and professional resource.

Never did Bryan make a purchase or sale on my behalf without first understanding my goals and risk tolerance level. It was always my decision made with more insight and assistance than I could possibly have possessed on my own. This is Guided Discovery™ working on my behalf. This accumulated guidance and instruction he has given me, and all of his clients over the years are now at my fingertips, a ready reference.

Reading this presentation of Bryan's is like having a refresher course in responsible money management, time tested and well confirmed by ultimate results.

I recommend this book to all readers with an interest in more responsible personal money management. Its precepts are well thought out, based on experience and demonstrably effective. I needed an advisor far more than I ever conceived and the principles that Bryan Sullivan presents here met and continue to meet my needs. It expanded my understanding and improved my investing strategy and it may well sharpen the reader's as well.

Based on my personal experience, I highly recommend this book to all who are considering working with a financial advisor and want to expand their own understanding and abilities in their personal financial management.

William J. Houston, Chaplain, U.S. Navy (Retired)

Table Of Contents

SECTION I

Are You Sabotaging Your Own Success?

CHAPTER 1

Introduction

The biggest fear most people face when planning for retirement is, **"Will my money last for my entire retirement?"** Unfortunately, people worry more about **if** their money is going to last than they worry about **how** their money is going to last.

There are many legitimate concerns that go into this fear: medical bills, housing costs, inflation, or helping children and grandchildren. Once retired, you may have twenty to forty years left to live and enjoy life. How are you going to maintain the lifestyle you enjoy? If you need to go back to work at seventy, who is going to hire you? What kind of work could you do?

In my opinion, people often are not only more concerned than necessary, they are concerned about the wrong things. The biggest fear people should have is, **"Am I protecting my money from myself?"**

To go from making a living to living on what your money is making is a new and often overwhelming experience for most people. This change often is compounded by other changes in their status quo – losing a spouse, for example. If that spouse has been primarily responsible for managing the couple's financial affairs – the one who paid the bills, managed the investments, and filed the tax returns – then the other spouse easily can become paralyzed. They are afraid, and rightly so.

At that point people often come to me and say, "I've never done any of this. I don't really understand any of it and, honestly, I'm scared to death to even try to learn how." That is when a financial advisor can provide an invaluable service: advice, strategy and hope. They have the knowledge and skills required to manage the many and complex variables associated with retirement and financial investments.

A good financial advisor can help you understand the real risks in managing your money and how to avoid them. At Vellum Financial, we help clients establish long term habits and strategies that will keep them on track and help them avoid making the mistakes so many others have made in their retirement.

Sometimes there is a learning curve, adjustments that have to be made, and even some pain, but in all cases **there is a solution**. What is important is whether or not you are ready to take on the learning curve and make whatever changes you need to make in order to make things work. Hopefully this book will help you understand the problems and the solutions so you can overcome your fears, meet your goals, and achieve peace of mind.

CHAPTER 2

"I Can Do It Myself!"

Why use an advisor to help manage your retirement money when you can do it yourself? Maybe you don't want somebody else to handle your money. Maybe you want to avoid the cost of doing business with an advisor.

I remember when I had just started working and bought my first house. My neighbor came by and said, "I want to buy this new wood burning fireplace insert. They will give me a great deal if I buy two of them. What do you think? Do you want to go in on this?"

Well, I lived up in Oregon at the time. The winters are cold there, my fireplace didn't produce much heat, and an insert really would help. It was a $1000 to buy this thing, and for a couple hundred more bucks they offered to send someone out to install it. So I paid the extra $200 to have it installed by a guy who did it every day. It got done, it looked great, and it worked great.

My next door neighbor was a "do-it-yourself" guy and he decided he was going to tackle the project himself. There was a step in the process when you had to drill through some metal. He didn't wear safety glasses while he was drilling it and a little metal shaving flicked into his eye. He had to go to the hospital and his sight was crippled for about three weeks. He was unable to drive and had to take time off work. Imagine the pain, agony, and expense he went through to save that $200.

Whether you pay someone to help you or you do it yourself there always will be a cost. It is important to weigh the cost of your time and the value of your abilities to manage your money as effectively as a trained professional who does it every day.

Most people don't spend their life managing money. There is more to it than just buying into a process and applying it, and there are many pitfalls that could cost you very dearly. When it's your money you also can't help being emotionally tied to it which can lead to even more mistakes. A good financial counselor is aware of these pitfalls and has experience providing assistance with almost every type of situation.

You should consider asking yourself,

"Am I willing to invest the time and energy to educate myself about money, and do I have the emotional fortitude to make the right decisions at the right times when I'm dealing with my own money?" These are very real and serious questions that a good financial advisor can help you work through.

For some of you the answer still may be, "Yes, I'm going to take the risk and do this myself." Many more of you will find that working with a qualified financial advisor provides more value.

It is unfortunate that so many people are more willing to risk managing their own money than they are willing to risk having somebody cut their lawn or paint their house. When it comes to their money they somehow think they are the expert and are afraid to give up control.

If somebody messes up my lawn it's not going to be the end of the world. It will grow back and I can get someone else to do it or cut it myself next week.

It doesn't work like that with money. If you make a mistake with your retirement money you can't ever get it back because your earning power is gone.

By hiring a financial advisor you are not

giving up control of your money. You still have the final say in how your investments are managed, how much risk you take and how much loss or gain you are willing to accept or try to achieve. These things all remain in your control. Your financial advisor is there to help you protect your standard of living by protecting your money from yourself.

CHAPTER 3

Are You Too Emotionally Attached To Your Money?

Everybody is affected differently by their emotions, but almost everybody is emotionally attached to their money. Managing retirement money is so vitally important to your well being that it is almost impossible not to be emotionally attached to it.

Unfortunately, one of the primary ways you can sabotage your financial success is acting upon your emotions. A financial advisor will help you avoid this trap. They will counsel you, advise you on the best methods, and talk you through issues so that you understand the risks and potentials in each situation.

As an example, let's say I'm seventy years old and I think I'm going to live another thirty years. I have a million dollars in my retirement account and I believe that will last me the rest of my life. Even if I earn 0% interest, I can take out $33,000 dollars a year for the next thirty years.

There are many other variables that can come into play, sometimes very quickly. Let's say I take out $33,000 the first year and everything goes great but the next year my investments drop from $1,000,000 in value to $800,000 dollars in value.

If I continue following that same plan, my money is not going to last, and what happens if I screw up and live longer? What happens if I have the same experience next year and I lose value in my investments? Do I take on more risks? Do I change what I need in terms of income?

You could be cold hearted and say, "I'm going to be dead. I don't really care what happens after I'm gone." But that is rarely the case. Most people are very concerned with their immediate spouse and many have an interest in leaving a legacy for their children and grandchildren.

This is especially true for couples. I talk to couples all the time where one of them is very concerned about making sure that their spouse will be able to take care of themselves for the rest of their life. For example, if I am seventy years old, married, and responsible for managing the money, I feel an obligation to take care of my spouse, not only as long as I'm alive but also as long as she is alive. I'm very emotionally tied to that idea and it will drive my decision-making process.

In addition, people often make decisions based on leaving enough money to help their grandkids go to college, for example, or making sure that their kids get to pay off their houses because that's what their parents did for them. These decisions are not right or wrong but they are large "emotionally-driven" decision-making factors, and these sometimes get in the way of making rational financial decisions.

Unfortunately, the way our retirement system works doesn't help. When one spouse dies Social Security decreases and sometimes a pension could evaporate completely. These factors all play into emotional decision-making.

When emotions take over the decision-making process easily can go awry. The investment fundamentals and financial information that an advisor has to offer get lost in the process.

An advisor helps to identify and define what you value in terms of retirement, money, freedom, flexibility, and travel. These all are things that an advisor looks at to help you match your goals and means with the right investment strategy and to develop a disciplined process that

is based on the greatest probability for your success.

CHAPTER 4

If You Know You Should Buy Low and Sell High, Then Why Don't You?

Almost everybody knows that to be successful in investing you have to buy low and sell high. That may seem to be overly simplified, but it is logical and sound.

So why do people let their emotions prevent them from following this rule? When a stock starts to run and the price goes way, way up, it is easy to get emotionally high and think it is going to run forever. Conversely, when a stock takes a turn and goes down, down, down, it is easy to get emotionally frustrated and think it will never come back.

As an example, let's say I have an investor who has ten stocks in a portfolio. Over time some of those did very well and some of them did poorly. The investor then begins to systematically sell the ones that are doing poorly and buy more of the ones that are doing well. He sells the dogs and buys more of the winners.

Intuitively, that seems to make sense. However, this behavior created the activity of selling low and buying high (Just the opposite of what we should be doing).

Once you go back and measure the results over time, those decisions would seem to have been made prematurely. If you are buying investments as they are going up, you generally are not getting the best values. Conversely, when you sell stocks because they are going down, and it is a decision based on price rather than investment fundamentals or technical reasons, then you're doing the opposite of selling high.

An advisor will help you make decisions based on a disciplined strategy that you previously agreed makes the most sense to achieve significant returns over time.

Significant doesn't have to be the difference between a 5% return and a 50% return. Significant is really a matter of a few percentage points. A difference of two or three percent return over time makes a very significant difference in your ability to make your money last.

Here is another example of taking emotion out of financial management. In 2008 we had a credit crisis that drove us into a very deep and significant recession. It started with the failure of one financial institution. Consequently, there was massive merger activity among banks that didn't know if they were going to be able to stay in business or not.

We then saw a mass exodus out of the stock market. Stock prices fell rapidly and my experience is that 98% of that was emotionally driven. Clients in March of 2009 were at close to panic levels, "I want to get out of the market. What if it goes to zero? I don't want to be the guy standing here holding onto it. I can't afford to lose anymore, how am I going to support myself, I'll have to go back to work . . ." All kinds of fears surfaced and all of these fears were based on emotional responses.

These people were asking the wrong questions. The questions they should have been asking are, "Am I properly allocated to get through this process?" and "Is there opportunity here to take advantage of buying low?"

There is a quote that has been mentioned many times in the last couple years by Warren Buffet that says, "Be fearful when others are greedy and be greedy when others are fearful." That concept has always proven to be true.

As an example, let's say that I go to the

grocery store to buy a can of beans. They normally sell for two dollars a can but today they are on sale for 25 cents a can and you can buy as many as you want. Instead of saying, "Oh, wow, the price just dropped dramatically. I'm not touching those beans," I say, "Back the truck up and buy as many cans as possible right now."

The flip side would be when I need a gallon of milk. At the local convenience store a gallon of milk normally sells for four or five dollars. If today they are selling it for nine dollars I'm not going to get two gallons just because I happen to be there and it's convenient. I'm going to get only what I need because the price is high.

I believe we should think about our investments in the same way. Buy more when prices are low…It's a more logical approach.

Timing, of course, is critical. To the untrained eye the timing of things may not be so apparent, but there are many professional firms in the stock market that are paid to fully understand timing. The signals for timing are there, but unfortunately the individual investor has the odds stacked against them in terms of being on the right side of the whole timing issue.

There's an old saying, "Time in the market not timing the market is where you're going to get your most value." There is great value in that statement but there also is some danger in how that is interpreted. The old philosophy of buy and hold has not worked very well over the last ten years.

The idea that you can just buy an S&P 500 fund and hold it over time and average 12% rate of return is no longer true. It may have been true for the eighties or the nineties, but in the last decade that has not been the case. If "buy & hold" was your philosophy the last decade, then you were lucky to have as much money at the end of ten years as you did when you started.

The major firms and most advisors spend their days looking at this stuff. They have pieces of information that have been gathered over time that can more than pay for whatever expense you incur by working with them.

CHAPTER 5

Is the Investment Environment Different Now Than in the Past?

I'm very careful about saying today is different than it ever was, but it is different. That is not to say that the financial situation won't ever be similar to what it was before, but there will be factors that are different.

It used to be that access to information was the differentiating component between those that were successful and those that weren't. That is not nearly as true today as it used to be because information is everywhere. Using the internet, anybody anywhere in the world can access the same information that any advisor has. Financial news stations inundate us with information 24 hours every day. So it is not the lack of information but the **interpretation** of that information today that helps us make the best decisions.

Today is also different because the availability of information aligns the world's economies much more closely – we instantly know what is going on in China and Japan and Europe and South Africa. When your mobile phone informs you that there has been an earthquake in Japan **as it is happening** you can't help but start reacting to fears of what that means and how it affects your investments.

The ability to get that information and to be nimble and proactively monitor it is great. But if I'm in retirement, do I want to get in my RV and travel around the country or go golfing or hop on a plane and go visit Europe or whatever I want to do? Or do I want to be spending my time sitting in front of a computer and monitoring a mobile phone for financial news? That is not retirement. That is work.

So why not take the work out of retirement and let somebody else help you? Not that you won't be readily available if your advisor calls. You certainly want to be informed and understand what is happening, but you probably don't want to be tied to the computer or the TV watching what's going on every moment.

Honestly, the challenge today is trying to **filter out the noise.** There is so much information available and so much of it is just plain noise. It doesn't really have any impact on what we may be doing in our investments today. Filtering the information is difficult unless you have had experience with the process. Unless you can step back from the whole experience, it is very difficult to see the forest through the trees. An advisor helps filter out the noise, put the good information into perspective, and help make sure you are not worrying about things that you really do not need to worry about.

CHAPTER 6

What Happens When Things Change?

Ideally, we would rather not need a contingency plan for market fluctuations. However, depending upon a number of factors – your risk tolerance, how much income you are taking from your investments, how much of that is necessary and how much is discretionary – you may want to have a back-up plan for dealing with the unexpected. Nonetheless, because there really are so many possibilities, in most cases we don't pre-design a contingency plan but apply a process to handle these fluctuations as they occur.

The year 2008 was very interesting because markets of all different types became very correlated. You may have heard the term "flight-to-quality." When the stock markets are misbehaving you sometimes can move your money to treasuries or short-term corporate bonds.

In the credit crisis of 2008, stocks were decimated, bonds got crushed, international investments were hammered, and some commodities suffered dramatically. There was no opportunity for a flight-to-quality. We had a situation where it was difficult to find a place to hide. Our contingency process always includes having a percentage of assets allocated to cash, and we actively monitor a situation like that to determine when it is time to increase our cash positions and how that is tied to the investors individual plan.

In 2008, we had between 20% and 25% allocated towards cash when the markets fell. By the middle of 2009 the indications were that it was time to start adding money into this. Our clients have been well rewarded for that. These decisions, if left to emotions, most likely would have dramatically different results.

SECTION II:

Using The Guided Discovery™ Process

CHAPTER 7

What Does Money Mean To You?

We strongly believe that a very large component of the overall investment management process has to do with helping clients identify what it is about money that is important to them. To help you articulate your attitudes towards money we use our Guided Discovery™ process.

Everybody is different. Attitudes towards money often stem from how we grow up. Whether our parents and grandparents were rich or poor greatly shapes our attitudes and values about money and forms our beliefs about what money can do and not do. It is very important for us as financial advisors to understand not only your goals and dreams for retirement but also where your fears and emotions get in the way of making logical and rational decisions regarding your money.

The Guided Discovery™ process helps

you to identify what it is you value about money which then helps us as advisors to identify where the potential pitfalls are for you as we go through the investment process. The other benefit is that it often helps us to uncover what it means for you to get the most out of your retirement.

I will give you a quick example. I had a couple that came in and went through this process, and we discovered that the woman had this dream as a little girl to go to Disneyland and she'd never had a chance. Life just got in the way. She got busy with their kids, they didn't live close enough and she basically never was able to make it a priority to go there.

One of the things we figured out was that to set them off in the right place in retirement we needed to plan their trip to Disneyland. She was 65 years old, and instead of spending her retirement worrying about standard deviation on a mutual fund or the beta on a particular stock, we said, "Let's take your values about what you want to do with your money and let's design a plan around that."

That's one of the best examples of what we really bring to this process. We help you to identify those types of things that are going to be important to you and then figure out the best way to manage and allocate your investments so that you can take the best advantage of them. That includes a component of understanding your fears and where are you going to potentially experience hiccups and make mistakes, but it also helps you to avoid them, and gives us the opportunity to help you enjoy more happiness.

We do have a questionnaire that we go through to help us identify what your timeframe is and your attitude towards risks, but the Guided Discovery™ process is really more of a consultative interview. We start by identifying what it is about money that's important to you. Then, if you are a couple, we walk each of you through it individually because we want to understand the dynamics of your different views.

There are different dynamics in every relationship. When we are managing money for a couple, for example, the wife could be a woman who has been very successful in business, who started her own firm, did a great job managing it, sold it, and made lots of money. Her husband might have been a midlevel accountant in corporate America and been successful in his own right, but is very conservative and very comfortable in the 9-5 environment working for somebody else. Their values and ideas about managing retirement may be very different. So we go through the Guided Discovery™ process with each of them to help discover their values.

We start out asking, "What is it about

money that's important to you?" Then we drill down from there. If you say flexibility or freedom, we ask, "What is it about flexibility or freedom that is important to you?" It may seem a little bit hokey but the conversation quickly gets very emotional.

I have had people in my office come to tears while uncovering the origins of their attitudes towards money. They say, "Wow, I didn't even realize that's where I was coming from." That is what I mean when I say this is an emotional process. These are very important components of managing your wealth. We help you find the source of your attitudes so that we can better serve your real interests. These are things that you will never discover by filling out a form online and sending your money to a web site.

Investment management and planning for retirement is so much more than putting together a spreadsheet. We ultimately become an outlet for how your emotions impact your money. Understanding your emotions towards money is truly an integral part of your investment management and decision-making process throughout the course of your retirement.

If it was a simple thing I could tell you that inflation is going to stay at 2% for the rest of your life and you can get 12% interest that's FDIC insured and completely liquid and give yourself a monthly check and have it compound and grow at the same time. There would be nothing to think about. If I knew all those things and I knew the day you were going to die, I could compute a retirement plan in three seconds and you would be out the door and I could put it online we would never even have to talk again. But that doesn't happen. That's not the real world.

The Real World: Recently Widowed

In the real world there are numerous components and influences and things that are going to happen after our working life is over that we're going to have to navigate through and we're going to have to make decisions on and some of those things are very, very important decisions. Being at that crossroad and making a choice, sometimes the facts are there and we can't see them or we can't identify with what are the actual consequences.

For an example, in one case we were able to help a gentleman who had been an iron worker for 40 years and had retired at age 59. At the time he was introduced to us he was 72 and had been retired for 13 years. He and his wife of 51 years had raised eight children. His entire working life he would come home on Friday and hand his paycheck to his wife. She managed their entire financial life even into retirement. The wife had passed away just three weeks before our initial meeting, and his biggest concern was that he hadn't ever written one check in his entire life. His wife had managed all of the finances.

Through our Guided Discovery™ process we were able to discover this man's complete dependency on his wife to handle the finances. The process revealed an ambivalent tolerance to risk, a deep commitment to his church, and a desire to help enhance his relationship with his children. Since retiring he spent most of his recreational time woodworking and doing projects around the house. Even though he had wanted to travel, he was unable to travel much due to his wife's health.

During the Guided Discovery™ process we discovered that he would enjoy spending more time traveling to visit the children and grandchildren, gaining an understanding of his finances and getting help managing his day-to-day financial needs, and finding ways to donate his passion for woodworking to his church and other organizations in the community.

We then performed a thorough financial review for this widower and provided a plan for him to achieve his goals. Together we agreed to analyze his past and projected spending, perform risk analysis, and reviewed his insurance coverage. In addition to implementing a tax-efficient, growth-oriented investment portfolio we began managing his monthly bill payment responsibilities and his mail and correspondence while he was traveling.

For his family we initiated the concept of yearly retreats and referred his family to best-in-class outfitters and travel agents who arranged all the detail; implemented technology solutions that included a family calendar, hosted e-mail, online portfolio reporting, and a secure document storage site; and coordinated with a tax advisor and an attorney to develop an updated estate plan.

We also provided payroll and screening services for his domestic help, coordinated his charitable giving, and compiled a list of charities and local organizations that offered an outlet to continue his passion for woodworking and cabinet making.

As a financial advisor I have already experienced 99% of the rest of your life through the lives of my other clients. I've already experienced the things you're going to experience in your retired life and the decisions and crossroads you're going to go through. I've helped you get your kids through school and college and weddings and I've worked with you as you've lost a spouse or a parent or helped someone put a parent into assisted living. I've gone through the process where both parents have died and the children have come in and we've helped figure out how those assets are going to be allocated. I've helped you with charitable intentions and identified the most efficient ways to establish those processes and put those assets in place. These are experiences that an advisor brings to the table that have real value and help provide a higher level of comfort when you come to those same crossroads in life.

CHAPTER 8

Developing A Family Wealth Mission Statement

One of the most valuable services we provided during the process of developing your financial plan is to develop your Family Wealth Mission Statement. This mission statement becomes the guiding concept for future decision-making.

The Real World: Family Business Transition

A matriarch and her husband of a successful family-owned business were approaching retirement. Two sons were working in the business, and the founder and her husband were looking forward to handing over the reins of the business, fishing, and enjoying time with their grandchildren. However, they were concerned about the inherent risk of family business transitions, the ability of their current investments to generate the necessary level of retirement income, and the structure of the business transition.

The Guided Discovery™ process confirmed our client's concerns about the business transition and uncovered the couple's overwhelming desire to see the business grow and become a legacy for future generations. The process also revealed a low risk tolerance and the need to maximize investment returns in order to achieve all desired goals. In addition, they were concerned with the risks to the business associated with divorce or death of either of the sons.

We began by helping the couple draft a comprehensive Family Wealth Mission Statement (FWMS), which contained a history of the family business, the couple's philosophy of wealth, their estate intentions, and their investment expectations. They felt so empowered and inspired by this process, they immediately shared the result with their children.

Using the Family Wealth Mission Statement as our road map, Vellum Financial performed a thorough financial review for the couple and implemented the necessary solutions to achieve their goals. We analyzed past and projected spending, performed risk analysis, reviewed insurance coverage, and coordinated with a tax advisor and an attorney to implement a values-driven estate plan. We then implemented a tax-efficient, growth-oriented investment portfolio with prudent exposure to alternative investments in order to enhance returns; took over monthly bill payment responsibilities; managed mail and correspondence while the couple traveled; provided payroll and screening services for domestic help; and coordinated charitable giving.

For the family we facilitated meetings where the Family Wealth Mission Statement was introduced and the estate plan reviewed and helped draft and implement family-business governance policies; implemented technology solutions that included a family calendar, hosted e-mail, online portfolio reporting, and a secure document storage site; developed cursory financial plans and investment management for both children; and compiled a list of charities that appealed to family's desire for charitable involvement that would get themselves and their grandchildren involved.

For the business we helped establish an independent board of directors and initiated formal owner/manager education requirements and career tracks for family employees. We reviewed existing ownership transition plans and suggested modifications that would augment retirement income while saving on transfer taxes.

SECTION III:

Will You Have Enough Money When You Retire?

CHAPTER 9

From Making A Living To Living On What You Made

We grew up seeing our parents work for their money and then we worked for our money most of our lives. From an early age we learned the value of making money by getting a paper route or mowing lawns in the neighborhood. Some of us babysat or maybe we received an allowance for doing chores at home.

Upon retirement that process stops all together. We stop working for our money. It is time to make our money work for us, but our schools and universities don't do a very good job of teaching us how.

The other day I read in the newspaper that more people forty-five years and younger believe in UFO's than believe they are going to receive Social Security in retirement. Pensions are going away and we now have so many problems with unfunded pensions that people in their twenties, thirties and forties recognize that they will not be able to depend on them. At some point they will need to have their money working for them.

That is a paradigm shift from our parents' generation and their parents' generation. They had a much greater dependence on pensions and Social Security. They also had the attitude that we work for our money, and that when we run out of money we can just go work for more. We know, of course, that it's not like that anymore.

My dad was a school teacher so he knew he'd have a little pension when he retired. He knew that in the worst case scenario he always would have at least something coming in. That was their "guaranteed retirement income." Unfortunately, as a percentage of our cost of living, that "guaranteed retirement income" is becoming much less significant as a component of what we need. So we need to think more about how we're going to make our money work effectively for us.

One of the biggest paradigm shifts in retirement is learning that you no longer supply your needs by the work of your hands. It is your previous work that is providing for your needs. This is a very critical shift in thinking. We all go through different struggles and trials in our working life but on any given day we can always pick ourselves up by our bootstraps and say, "Alright, let's just get back out there and find a way to make some money." In retirement we lose that ability and become reliant on our financial assets to carry us and do those things for us.

CHAPTER 10

What's Your Number?

What will your retirement lifestyle look like? The answer goes much deeper than how much money you will have.

We don't say, "Give me your money, I'm going to invest it and then we'll figure out what you need to do." We first ask, "Where are you at right now? What are your goals? Where do we need to go? What amount of money will provide that lifestyle and meet the financial needs you have or perceive to have?"

There's an ad on TV that asks, "What's your number?" We use that same concept. We develop your balance sheet and your income and expense statement. Then we look at what's going to change. What are the other anticipated expenses that you're going to have in retirement? Insurance, for example, is a big one. It's a wild card that we try to help you identify.

This is the same way I would analyze a business. I build a balance sheet that provides a clear picture of all your assets and debts so that we can know what your financial situation looks like today. What do you own? What is it worth? How liquid is it? What is your 401K worth? Do you have IRA's? Do you have annuities? Do you have CD's or savings accounts? Do you have investment accounts? What are those worth? How about real estate? Do you own your home or do you have a mortgage?

Then I build an income and expense statement. People usually don't already have these prepared so part of our process is to create them and organize them in a way that is going to help you get a clear financial picture.

We ask you, "What does your Social Security check look like? Do you have pensions? What are your investments paying currently? What's your mortgage? What's your rent? What are your utility expenses and what are your travel goals? Are you going to join the country club and start playing golf every week and what's that cost? Do you have any anticipated windfalls of cash? Do you have elderly parents? Do you expect to receive some sort of inheritance over the next ten years, fifteen or twenty years?"

In many cases people don't really know the answers. They think things like, "My parents might have a million dollars today but my mom may get sick and spend it all." Nonetheless, it is important for us to develop a complete picture of your expectations and anticipations and plan from there.

If you were going to analyze a company's stock, the first two items you would look at would be cash flow (income and expense statement) and a balance sheet. We start our analysis of your financial health in the same way.

Many times people say, "Well I can live on less in retirement." Sometimes that is true. Some things may actually cost you less. You may have just paid your house off so you don't have the housing expense that you used to have. Many times a client comes to us and their house is paid for so they don't have a housing expense. They have property taxes and utilities, but their total housing expense is much less.

Those kinds of expenses may go down, but then leisure and health expenses tend to go up in retirement, at least for a while. Leisure may drop down again as you get into your late eighties and early nineties. You may not golf as much or travel as much as before, and your health expenses tend to go up and that can be a huge concern.

We help you identify your current picture

and what it may look like in the future. It is not an exact science but based on our discovery process we develop a plan with which everyone is comfortable. We put it all together and arrive at a number that represents how much money you need to have for your retirement to be workable.

Another one of the things you want to consider when planning your retirement is location. You may live in Boston and want to retire to Florida. The cost of living is actually cheaper in Florida than Boston. We also keep these things in mind and talk about different geographical areas.

For example, you may have bought your house thirty years ago in California and could sell it today for $1,000,000. You only have $200,000 in savings. Your children don't live at home anymore. You could move to Austin, Texas to be closer to the grandkids and buy a house for $150,000 and have it paid for, then put $700,000 dollars towards your retirement. That may then give you the lifestyle you desire and the ability to travel more and to do the things that you want to do. We talk about geographical options in an overall context and provide some examples.

CHAPTER 11

Probability Analysis Using Monte Carlo Simulation

There is an analysis tool called Monte Carlo simulation that we also use to evaluate your options. It is not perfect and is not a financial planning tool, but it gives us the ability to explore the potential hurdles that you are going to encounter in retirement. Monte Carlo stimulation takes every permutation and possibility of how investments have performed and could perform based on interest rate moves and market fluctuations and gives us a better idea of the probability that your money will last through your retirement. It is never 100% correct because there will always be situations for which we just cannot plan.

For example, drawing an income from your investments is going to make a significant difference. Let's say that I've got $500,000 and I need to take $1,000 dollars a month. If I start in 1991 it works great, but if I start it in 1999, ten years out I am upside down and it is not working.

Monte Carlo simulation looks at your assumed allocation and runs through every possible scenario to determine the probability a scenario will work based on your principal and draw rate.

It doesn't just stop there. Once you have done all these calculations and you've got your number we have to ask, "Does that work in all scenarios?"

If the answer is no, we have to understand why. What happens if you retire tomorrow and we have another October 2008 or we have another October 1987? What happens to your retirement if you're starting to draw income and you are already down 30% in the first two months? We try to accommodate every scenario.

I will give you another example. If you have five years of investment ahead and the first two years you are already down 10% each year, and the next three years you are up 10% each of those years, your average return over that time period is 2%. That's not great, but if I know that I'm going to average 2% and I can live off a 2% draw, that's great. The problem is if the first two years are down 10% each I may not be able to recover from that. Conversely if the first three years are up 10% each, I may be in great shape and may be able to absorb those 10% down years in the last two years.

For people that retired in January of 2007 and took all their money and put it into the S & P 500, by March of 2009 they were down 40%+ in value from where they had invested. Now their $1,000,000 life savings is $500,000 or $600,000 and they are wondering what to do.

It would be a very difficult situation for somebody who is managing their own money to say, "I'm just going to stay with this." The problem is, if you decide to pull the trigger and get out and just "go to the sidelines," when do you get back in? When things look better?

Let's say a year and a half later things are better. Is it time to get back in? Maybe it's too high now. So your mind starts to play tricks on you. We try to take those types of situations out of the equation. We want our clients to call us if they have concerns but we also want them to know and understand the methodology we use to manage their investments and how market moves are going to affect their portfolio.

If we need to make changes, adjustments or tweaks to it, we're going to advise you to do those things and we help you with that process. You already should have a plan in place that has considered the possibility of that happening and know that we have taken the steps to navigate and manage through that possibility already. We eliminate the need to make decisions based on fear and panic. Then we can make decisions based on knowing this was a possibility, that we have other investments that are working for us in this situation.

Knowing whether to make changes on underperforming investments or continue to hold them based on a plan and an investment discipline is a much better place to be than to be reactive to whatever happens to be going on in the economy or the world at any given moment.

CHAPTER 12

About Invading Principle

There are many different ways to look at it, but in an ideal world we would never touch our principal. Our principal would stay put and we could say, "I've got 10 million dollars. I only need $50,000 a year to live. If I stick this into a portfolio of municipal bonds that generate $250,000 a year, I can take $50,000 a year and reinvest the other $200,000 in something. I'll never touch my principal."

That would be wonderful. The other scenario is, "I have $500,000 in savings. I've got a small pension for $1500 and I've got a Social Security check for $1000. So I have $2500 dollars a month coming in and my expenses are $3500 dollars." That $500,000 has to make up the additional thousand dollars a month I need.

What happens if $1000 a month works when I'm sixty years old and by the time I'm eighty I may need $2000 dollars a month or $3000 dollars a month? The question then becomes, "How do I invest that $500,000 in a way that I can actually grow it and still be able to give myself a raise at some point in the future?"

I always like to say, "Tell me when you're going to die and I can design an exact retirement plan for you." (humor intended) My dad used to say his idea of a retirement plan would be when we kids wrote the check to the mortician, it would bounce. He would have spent every single last penny that he had, but it would last until the day he died, no longer and no shorter, and that would be great. Of course, it never works that way. What happens if you screw up and live too long?

Invading principal is a concept that has many different facets to it. There are tools that are designed specifically for invading principal that have a component of insurance to them.

A pension plan is an example of this. I pay into my pension plan or my company pays into my pension plan for me for 40 years while I'm working, and it's set up so that it will pay me an income stream for the rest of my life. So it is designed to pay me out until I die, and after I die it stops; it is gone. In some cases it is a joint life plan so it pays myself and my spouse for the rest of our lives. If she outlives me then it will continue until she passes away, but then it stops.

There also are insurance companies that create annuity income streams that are designed to do just that, and you can actually take a lump sum of money and basically create a private pension plan. In some cases they are appropriate tools to be using in retirement but it is a calculated decision and there are consequences to those decisions that could be negative.

In 2011 you might say, "I can comfortably live on $5,000 a month." Then I could tell you to take your million dollar lump sum and buy you an annuity income of $5,000 dollars a month that lasts you the rest of your life. Then you might say, "Great, if I could do that I'm set for life."

That might work great in 2011, but over the next ten years as the dollar continues to devalue we might have a period of time like the seventies when we had inflation in the double digit range and suddenly the cost of gas is no longer $4 a gallon but has gone to $15 a gallon, and the cost of groceries is no longer $100 but $400 every time we to go the grocery store. Then that $5,000 a month may no longer foot the bills. If you buy an annuity stream, that's a risk that you take, and there is no way to go back and adjust that or dip into principal because you are   committed to that income stream.

Maybe for a portion of an investment pool it might make sense to dip into some principal

and make that commitment to buy yourself a life-
time pension as part of a security blanket. Maybe
we end up like Japan, and we have very low inflation for a very long period of time and that works
out fantastic. There are many things we don't
know so everything depends on what your needs
are, what your risk tolerances are, and how much
you are willing to give up.

For any decision you make in retirement
there is a trade off and you have to look at the
whole landscape. Your financial planning should
start with the Guided Discovery™ process to find
out what is it that you most value about money,
then follow where that takes you to determine
how invading principal plays into that whole picture.

SECTION IV:

Selecting A Financial Advisor

CHAPTER 13

Rapport, Trust, and Long Term Relationships

When you are ready to find somebody to help you manage your money, how do you decide whom to trust? The most important factor is going to be somebody with whom you have a very fundamental and strong rapport.

Of course you are going to need trust, but trust doesn't come immediately; it happens over time. So to get started with an advisor you first are have to start with rapport.

Life is too short to be working with somebody you don't like. A financial advisor may be the smartest person in the world and can help you get excellent returns, but when you call them to talk about how much money you should spend on your daughter's wedding and you get rubbed the wrong way, that's not the person you want to be managing your life savings.

The first thing to put in the back of your mind before you even start your search is that you want to find somebody with whom you can connect, somebody who really understands you, understands your family, takes some interest in your livelihood so that when you do start to make decisions they can help you to make those important decisions. Some type of affinity or strong rapport is the foundation.

There are a couple of ways you can go about it. I love the idea of referrals. Talking with somebody you trust and respect that has a good relationship with somebody they work with is always a good starting point. However, I always recommend talking to many different people. We sometimes have a tendency to say, "Oh, something happened to my car, where do you get your car fixed? . . . Okay, I'll take it over there," or, "My cleaning lady just quit, who do you use?"

With a financial advisor you need to take it one step further. I would suggest asking for a referral but also interview several more advisors to get a real sense of how they manage the process until you find the one with whom you are going to have the best rapport and long term relationship.

Once you get to the point where you are interviewing, also look for things that will matter to you in the long run. What is their availability?

What is their policy on returning calls or giving you an appointment? What is their investment discipline? How will they help you make those decisions? Their answers need to not only make sense but also to resonate with you.

If you are an engineer and very structured you may want to know a lot more detail. The advisor should be able to explain the process to you, what technologies they are using to help them manage your money and specifically how they make buying and selling decisions.

I believe that every financial advisor also should bring up the issue of compensation. Are they fee-based advisors, commission-based advisors, flat fee advisors or hybrids? I will discuss the differences in the next section.

There also are designations to look at such as education and experience that an advisor brings to the table that help make them valuable to you. You sometimes read in money magazines that you only should hire a CFP. Most people don't even know what a CFP is or what it means or what criteria are required to qualify to get and keep that designation. Designations can be important but having somebody with long term experience is more important than almost any type of designation anybody can have.

You want to work with someone who has

experience in the area that you need advice. If my specialty is managing money for retirees, and you come to me about funding a small business and I don't have experience in that area, I am not the right person to help you with that. Similarly, a small business funding expert is not the person you want handling your retirement investments. It is best to have an advisor that has experience with the types of things that will come up in your life. When they do, your advisor will understand and be able to help you better.

Ultimately, it is not so much about the advisor selling you on his or her expertise as it is about you finding the "right fit". The crux of a successful relationship with your financial advisor is the relationship. You have the power in the relationship, and the advisor should have to do a really good job of proving to you that they are the right fit. One person may want the type of advisor that is all business, too busy managing your money and doing well for you. Another person may want somebody who is more open to meeting in person, answering many questions and giving advice about money. It really is a personal preference.

Some people may think they are more concerned about performance, but in the long term, the relationship is the key. I am not trying to discount performance, but the baseline has to be the relationship and performance is a component of that. Any advisor may have a great track record for five to ten years, but there will always be a hiccup along the way. If the client and advisor don't have a good working relationship that can navigate through that storm, it will be virtually impossible to have a long term relationship.

CHAPTER 14

Why Fee-Based Advisors Are Your Best Friend

There three basic ways an advisor gets paid. There are some hybrid models as well, but the traditional way financial advisors get paid is through a commission process. In my opinion there are some very fundamental flaws in that process. It is still very common today to pay a commission for a stock purchase or sale. So when a broker suggest that you sell stocks to purchase other stocks, you pay a commission to sell those stocks and pay another commission for the stocks you purchase.

Whether those investments are profitable or not, the advisor gets paid. So, in my opinion, there is a fundamental conflict of interest in that activity. The more activity in that account, the more the advisor gets paid. Even if the advisor has done all the right things and gives you the very best advice possible, there is an inherent conflict of interest because the advisor's compensation is tied directly to short term activity and not to the long term performance of your investments.

There has been a movement away from that model and towards a fee-based model over the last ten years or so. This has become more popular because it puts the advisor on the same side of the table as the client.

In the fee-based model the advisor's fee is calculated as a percentage of the value of the account. The plus side for you as a client is that the advisor's financial incentive is the same as yours. You both want your investments to increase in value. For the advisor to make more money he has to make more money for you.

The fee-based advisor has the least conflict of interest because compensation is tied to performance regardless of the number of trades that are done in an account. It is a win/win situation. Although the advisor still gets paid if your investments decrease in value, the fee paid also decreases. So there is an inherent disincentive for bad performance, and this helps to drive the advisors thinking process in your favor more than getting paid per transaction.

Advisors are required to tell you how they get compensated and fee structures are usually found in the fine print of your contract. A problem with the commission-based model is that many financial products have been created whose commissions are not totally transparent. Often it can be difficult to know for sure how those fees work. Therefore it may not be clear on your statement exactly what fees you paid.

A fee-based advisor clearly defines those fees on your statement. It is very transparent. Your contract with the advisor clearly defines those fees, and that fee arrangement is filed with the SEC.

CHAPTER 15

When You Should Change Advisors

About half of our current clients had a relationship with another advisor prior to working with us and there can be many reasons why someone might change advisors. Sometimes the reason is performance related. When that's the case it certainly does make sense to shop around. If you are not happy with the performance you are getting, either your advisor has not done a good job or they haven't adequately explained what's happening.

Sometimes people become unhappy because of a lack of communication. Surprisingly enough, there are many advisors who don't return calls until days later. If you aren't getting the time and attention you need, then it may be time to start looking for somebody that will provide it.

There are also advisors who will flat out tell you, "I'm not going to call you back. I manage money and that's what I do. Somebody on my staff will be happy to answer questions for you regarding your deposits, dividends, and statements." As long as you understand and agree to those rules it is fine. In many cases, however, we have found that people look for a new advisor because they are looking for a different experience.

Another reason people change advisors is due to what I refer to as money in motion. That is when many things happen at once to change the status quo. For example, when parents pass away and leave a substantial inheritance. If you didn't have a lot of money and were working with somebody with whom you haven't been impressed, then you may want to talk to someone who is well qualified to help you make that transition and manage your larger investment.

Another example might be getting transferred. Your job changes and you move across country. Although you still have a 401K to manage, you may not have a strong connection with your old advisor, so it is time to shop around for another.

As you can see, there are many legitimate reasons to change advisors. It is your money so it is up to you to decide if and when it right for you to seek a change.

CHAPTER 16

Conclusion

How are you going to make the transition from making money to making your money work for you? How are you going to make your money last?

Although there are many legitimate fears you might have about your money and retirement, I am hoping that this short book has provided you with some ideas on how to answer these questions, alleviate your worries some, and helped you to begin to understand how to meet your retirement goals.

Financial management does not have to be a daunting task. In fact, for most people the most financially responsible and rewarding solution is to hire a professional. If you truly understand the risks involved, enjoy the daily task of monitoring markets and money, can maintain emotional distance and adhere to a plan when making decisions, then managing your money yourself may be the best solution for you.

If, however, you are not in a position to education yourself and maintain the level of awareness and distance required to protect your money from yourself, hiring an advisor has many benefits.

As you get older, managing money doesn't get any easier, and the changes that challenge your well being – losing your spouse, illness, medical needs, etc. -- only make it more difficult. It is easy to lose sight of your plan and become paralyzed or, maybe worse, make the wrong decisions.

Although my practice and most of my clients are located in California, I have been practicing for twenty years have clients nationwide. Some of the relationships I have developed over the years are very strong. As people have moved away they have continued to do business with me and referred me to their new friends. I have some clients I have never met face-to-face because that person was referred to me by one of my clients.

The types of clients with whom I tend to have the best relationships are either retired already or are just about to move into retirement. They are trying to understand the concept of protecting their money from themselves. They haven't quite identified with that terminology or that idea, but there is that fear factor in them and they know this is a big undertaking. Sometimes they already have been retired for a while and had an experience they wasn't comfortable. Whatever the reason may be, they are identifying with the idea of protecting their hard-earned money from themselves and working with an advisor that can help them.

Working with retirees and people just coming into retirement is almost all I do. It is not uncommon for a couple in their sixties to have parents in their eighties pass away and suddenly have an inheritance with which they have no idea what to do. They may know there are some things they should do but need advice about what makes the best sense at this point in their life.

Or maybe they are in position where a parent has to move into a nursing home and they need help managing their parent's money. They want to understand how that whole process works and what is the best way to manage that money. There is so much cash going out to pay for their parent's expenses that they are looking for solutions that will alleviate their fears about managing the money and making it last. These are the types of clients with whom our firm does its best work because of our vast experience working with similar clients in the past.

In the beginning of my firm's relationship with a new client we try to have a face-to-face meeting. With today's technology, it's also easy for us to arrange a web based video meeting. The first appointment is an introduction to who we are, what we do, the kinds of clients we work with, and we go through the Guided Discovery™ process. We get to know you and your values so that we can understand who you are and what you need. We then analyze your financials, bank statements, brokerage statements, and tax returns. At a follow up meeting within a week to ten days we go over your balance sheet and income & expense statement. We show you our initial plan based on all the information we learned in our first meeting and your financial information.

At that point you choose whether to engage with us or not. If you are still in the interview process and comparing several advisors we let you take this information home and sleep on it and discuss it amongst yourselves.

Financial advisors usually do a really great job of selling themselves, telling you how they are going to manage your money and how they are going to keep in contact with you. Unfortunately their execution is not always as smooth as they outlined. One of the things we do is run our practice much like my dentist runs his. Every time we have an appointment, whether it's a phone appointment or a face-to-face appointment, we schedule the next follow up. It may be a re-view next month, in sixty days, or a year, but we schedule the next appointment before you leave the current appointment so that we share mutual expectations about our next contact. We hope to keep our clients engaged in what we are doing so we send out a regular schedule of statements, per-formance reports, newsletters and other commu-nications. We also maintain a blog to keep our clients up-to-date online.

There are many reasons to be afraid, but you don't have to be. Follow the recommenda-tions of this book. Research the financial advisors available to you. Ask your friends for references. Talk to each advisor to learn how they work and will manage your money, but also look to find the best fit for you. Find an advisor you like, with whom you can easily achieve rapport, and then trust them to help you learn and plan and move forward with confidence. Money is truly impor-tant, but peace of mind is invaluable.

If it makes sense for you, I am hoping Vellum Financial will be on your list of advisors to interview. We make our living by helping you improve your financial position so that you can live and enjoy your life. Wherever your road may take you, I wish you the best for a happy and joyous retirement.

APPENDICES

APPENDIX A:

Case Studies

The Retired Couple

Situation
The client is a couple who have been retired for five years. They built significant wealth while he was a corporate executive for a public company. The couple had been using several investment advisors but was not certain they were getting the results they desired. They have four children and six grandchildren. They love to travel and split their time between homes in North Carolina and Phoenix. He is an avid golfer and she loves to play tennis and spend time with the grandchildren. They have been generally happy with the tax and estate advisors they have in place but are concerned about the coordination and management of their financial affairs. They sometimes feel overwhelmed with the amount of paperwork with which they are constantly dealing, and both are intrigued by the potential to consolidate the work with a full-service multi-client family office.

Process
Vellum Financial's Guided Discovery™ process uncovered several interesting things. Both husband and wife had an unfulfilled desire to make a difference in the world. His goal is to provide business incubation scholarships to small start-up entrepreneurs. She would like to provide help in addressing social and educational issues of abused children. They wanted to dedicate time

and resources to these issues, while still maintaining the flexibility to travel and use their homes. Their estate plan was well-crafted but required some improvement to accommodate their newly disclosed interest in philanthropy. A series of other priorities also emerged during our Guided Discovery™ process: spending more time with family, outsourcing the tedious day-to-day financial tasks, exploring private aircraft ownership, and caring for an aging parent with chronic illness.

Execution

- Helped the client draft a Family Wealth Mission Statement (FWMS) which communicates their general philosophy of wealth, estate intentions, charitable intentions, and investment expectations.

- Undertook a complete portfolio review using the mission statement as a road map. As a result, one manager was retained, two were replaced, and complementary investments were added to build out a completely diversified portfolio.

- Worked with existing advisors to craft an integrated estate plan that dovetailed perfectly with the couple's charitable intentions; this new plan ultimately will generate more wealth for all involved – the couple, their heirs, and their charitable beneficiaries.

- Established a private foundation to fund current charitable activities and engage children and grandchildren in the process.

- Funded a charitable remainder trust (CRT) with low basis stock; the couple will use annuity payments to fund life insurance premiums, while the remaining interest will further fund the private foundation.

- Took over bill payment and bookkeeping for primary and secondary residences, delivering monthly reports on expenses to the owners.

- Coordinated the activity of property managers and household help at second homes.

- Conducted a complete risk assessment and reviewed existing insurance risks; identified and addressed areas of excessive exposure; and consolidated insurance to a central carrier to get better coverage at institutional prices.

- Implemented a mail management solution that enables client to receive a daily e-mail summary of correspondence.

- Designed technology solutions that included Web access to family travel calendars, central document storage, and online investment reporting.

- Initiated the concept of yearly family retreats; referred the family to best-in-class outfitters and travel agents who arranged all the details.

- Researched and made recommendations regarding private aircraft ownership opportunities including fractional ownership.

- Introduced the client to medical resources who could coordinate care for the aging parent, including a dedicated medical advocate to oversee care.

- Arranged for the production of a family biography, which included video interviews with the client's parents.

- Planned and facilitated family meetings, where the Family Wealth Mission Statement was first introduced, the estate plans were reviewed, and specific family goals were set.

- Facilitated ongoing meetings relating to a private foundation and the family's philanthropic efforts

If You Are Retired, or Close To Retiring,
Schedule A **FREE** Consultation With
Bryan Now By Calling **1-800-546-0123**

You can obtain a free retirement guide online at:
http://www.VellumFinancial.com/freeguide

The Entrepreneur

Situation
The husband of a couple in their late forties has been very focused on building his business, which he owns equally with a partner. His wife helps out in the business and has been busy raising three kids – one now in college, and two in high school. The couple's investable assets are small, relative to the size of the business. They want to get the most out of their current investments, while preparing for a potential sale of the business within five years.

Process
Vellum Financial's Guided Discovery™ process revealed that the couple was concerned about more than their investment performance. Both worried about the effect that affluence is having on their kids. They missed the closeness of their family when the children were younger, and had different ideas about inheritance plans. A review of current documents revealed potential problems with the partner's buy/sell agreements, a lack of coordination between business and estate plans, and opportunities to improve business performance and prepare for its sale.

Execution

- Coordinated comprehensive investment management across taxable accounts and company-sponsored 401(k) holdings; introduced alternative asset classes, such as private equity and absolute return to enhance risk/return profile.

- Implemented tax-saving strategies for college funding.

- Coordinated a comprehensive estate plan with the business partner.

- Worked with the existing insurance broker to consolidate and improve life insurance policies backing up their buy/sell agreements.

- Facilitated annual valuations for company.

- Initiated a strategic planning process for the business that identified and prioritized steps needed to prepare business for sale.

- Helped the client implement a new employee compensation and bonus plan that tied bonuses to performance.

- Assisted the family in establishing a donor-advised fund and developed a family gifting plan involving the children; generated tax savings by funding this with appreciated stock.

- Facilitated a family meeting where the estate

plan was introduced and family philanthropy goals were established.

- Helped the family research and plan an annual summer vacation.

- Identified a unique charitable interest of each family member and then sourced a related volunteer opportunity that the family could do together.

- Provided college-age child with internship opportunities through our internship program.

If You Are An Entrepreneur, Schedule A **FREE** Consultation With Bryan Now By Calling **1-800-546-0123**

You can also obtain a free money guide online at: **http://www.VellumFinancial.com/freeguide**

The Family Business Transition

Situation

The matriarch and her husband of a successful family-owned business were approaching retirement. Two sons were working in the business, and the founder and her husband were looking forward to handing over the reins of the business, go fishing, and spend more time with their grandchildren. However, they were concerned about the inherent risk of family business transitions, the ability of their current investments to generate the necessary level of retirement income, and the structure of the business transition.

Process

Vellum Financial's Guided Discovery™ process confirmed the client's concerns about the business transition and uncovered the couple's overwhelming desire to see the business grow and become a legacy for future generations. The process also revealed a low risk tolerance and the need to maximize investment returns in order to achieve all desired goals. In addition, they were concerned with the risks to the business associated with the divorce or death of either of their sons.

Engagement

We began by helping the couple draft a comprehensive Family Wealth Mission Statement (FWMS), which contained a history of the family business, the couple's philosophy of wealth, their estate intentions, and their investment expectations. They felt so empowered and inspired by this process, they immediately shared the result with their children. Using the FWMS as our road map, Vellum Financial performed a thorough financial review for the couple and implemented the necessary solutions to achieve their goals:

- Analyzed past and projected spending.

- Performed risk analysis and review of all insurance coverage.

- Coordinated with their tax advisor and attorney to implement a values-driven estate plan.

- Facilitated family meetings where the mission statement was introduced and the estate plan reviewed.

- Helped draft and implement family-business governance policies.

- Helped the business establish an independent board of directors.

- Initiated formal owner/manager education requirements and career tracks for family employees.

- Reviewed existing ownership transition plans and suggested modifications that would augment retirement income while saving on transfer taxes.

- Took over monthly bill payment responsibilities.

- Managed mail and correspondence while couple traveled.

- Provided compliant payroll and screening services for domestic help.

- Implemented tax-efficient, growth-oriented investment portfolio with prudent exposure to alternative investments in order to enhance returns.

- Implemented technology solutions that included a family calendar, hosted e-mail, online portfolio reporting, and a secure document storage site.

- Developed cursory financial plans and investment management for both children.

- Compiled list of charities that appealed to family's desire for charitable involvement that you could get themselves and their grandchildren involved.

- Coordinated charitable giving.

If You Are Part of a Family Business, Schedule A
FREE Consultation With Bryan Now By
Calling **1-800-546-0123**

You can also obtain a free money guide online at:
http://www.VellumFinancial.com/freeguide

The Recent Widower

Situation
This gentleman had been an iron worker for forty years and had retired at age 59. At the time we met he was 72 and had been retired for thirteen years. He and his wife of fifty years had raised eight children. His entire working life he would come home on Friday and hand his paycheck to his wife. She managed their entire financial life even into retirement. The wife had passed away just three weeks before our initial meeting, and his biggest concern was that he had never written a check in his entire life. His wife had managed all of the finances.

Process
Our Guided Discovery™ process uncovered this gentleman's complete dependency on his wife regarding finances. The process revealed an ambivalent tolerance to risk, a deep commitment to his church, and a desire to enhance his relationship with his children. Since retiring he spent most of his recreational time woodworking and doing projects around the house. Even though he had wanted to travel, he was unable to travel much due to his wife's health. A series of other priorities also emerged during our Guided Discovery™ process: spending more time traveling to visit the children and grandchildren, gaining an understanding of his finances, getting help managing his day-to-day financial needs, and finding

ways to donate his passion for woodworking to his church and other organizations in the community.

Execution
Vellum Financial performed a thorough financial review for the widower and implemented these solutions to achieve his goals:

- Analyzed past and projected spending.

- Performed a risk analysis and review of all insurance coverage.

- Took over monthly bill payment responsibilities.

- Managed mail and correspondence while traveling.

- Provided compliant payroll and screening services for domestic help.

- Implemented tax-efficient, growth-oriented investment portfolio with prudent exposure to alternative investments in order to enhance returns.

- Coordinated charitable giving.

- Initiated the concept of yearly family retreats. Referred family to best-in-class outfitters and travel agents who arranged all the details.

- Coordinated with a tax advisor and attorney to implement updating estate plan.

- Facilitated family meetings where the Family Wealth Mission Statement was introduced and the estate plan reviewed.

- Implemented technology solutions that included a family calendar, hosted e-mail, on-line portfolio reporting, and a secure document storage site.

- Developed cursory financial plans and investment management for all three children.

- Compiled a list of charities and local organizations that offered an outlet to continue his passion for woodworking and cabinet making.

If You Have Recently Lost A Spouse and Need Assistance With Sorting Out Financial Details, Please Schedule a **FREE** Consultation With Bryan Now By Calling **1-800-546-0123**

APPENDIX B:

Resources

Paytrust - http://www.paytrust.com

This all-in-one online bill pay service allows you to easily receive, track, and pay all your bills online. This is one of my favorite sites. I've been using this service for almost 8 years now.

Basically, you set up an account, and have all of your bills (mortgages, credit card bills, utilities, etc.) sent to your own personal P.O Box, and they receive your physical mail every day. They open it, scan it, and then will automatically pay your bills from the account you specify. You can even set limits, so if my credit card bill is $500 or less, I have them pay it automatically, but if it's more than $500, then they will send me an email and I have to confirm that everything is ok before it gets paid.

It's a fabulous service for the price, and if you're retired and travel a lot, or if you just want someone else to manage this process for you, then it's a great deal. The best part is that all of your bills are digitally stored for you as long as you keep your account.

The Daily Show - http://www.thedailyshow.com

You'll hear me often say, "Stop Watching The News - It's Just Noise". The Daily Show is a satirical television program airing each Monday through Thursday on Comedy Central. Jon Stewart took over as host in January 1999, making the show more strongly focused on politics and the national media. It is currently the longest running program on Comedy Central and makes me laugh at how ridiculous our news really is. A definite must to help us all keep the "news" in perspective.

Investopedia - http://www.investopedia.com

This includes the most comprehensive investing dictionary on the web as well as articles and tutorials on just about everything financial related.

Mint - http://www.mint.com

Mint brings all your financial accounts together online and automatically categorizes your transactions, lets you set budgets and helps you achieve your savings goals.

This site has been around for a couple years now and is constantly getting better. It's like an online version of Quicken, and it's free.

For the tech savvy individuals, it now has mobile apps to let you view a comprehensive picture of your finances right on your phone.

There is built in analysis that will give you suggestions and referrals to financial services that can save you money...like discount brokerages, or mortgage companies with great interest rates.

Bank Rate - http://www.bankrate.com

Compare mortgage, refinance, insurance and CD rates. Expert analysis of home loan finance topics and trends.

I love this site for anytime I'm trying to get a handle on what a good rate is. If I'm helping someone analyze their mortgage, or reduce the debt service on a credit card, this site is a great resource for comparison rate shopping.

College Savings Calculator –
http://www.savingforcollege.com/college-savings-calculator

Most Financial Advisors will have access to fairly sophisticated college planning software. In fact, if you tell me that you have 2 kids that are age 4 and 7, and you want the older one to attend Harvard, and the younger one to attend BYU. I have software that can tell me the exact cost of tuition, room, board, and misc items today, and then project the cost based on current college inflation rates, and I'll be able to tell you exactly what the cost of sending your two kids to college will be.

Then we back into what your current savings is, how much you want to pay for, how much financial aid (if any), we think they'll be able to get, and what we need to put away each month/year to get you there.

Well, this tool isn't quite that sophisticated, but it does a great job of giving you a sense of what it's going to take. And there's some other good advice for parents to think about with regards to 529 plans and custodial accounts.

Wedding Budget Calculator –
http://www.ourdreamwedding.com/index.cfm?page=wedding_budget_form_1&crid=7

Flowers? Dress? Center Pieces? Food? Rehearsal Dinner??? It's all so overwhelming... I know this is a long link, but if you're just trying to get a quick handle on what you can afford to spend on what.

This page will allow you to put in your total budget for a wedding, and it will spit back a list of items to consider with a dollar amount that would be appropriate for your particular budget.

Morningstar – http://www.morningstar.com

A great way to compare mutual funds and ETF's. They have their own proprietary research as well. If you read about a fund and want to learn more about it, Morningstar is the default place to go to find out more.

Yahoo Finance - http://finance.yahoo.com

This is a site I use every day. It's a comprehensive snapshot of the market, and when I want to drill down on a particular company or mutual fund, it's easy to just type in a symbol and find out an enormous amount of information. You can easily run charts and compare companies look up what the street thinks about your stock, or take a look at the latest quarterly report.

The Street – http://www.thestreet.com

This sight is pretty well laid out, and offers a lot of timely information. It's partially owned by CNBC infotainment celebrity, Jim Cramer. Although I'm not a huge Cramer fan, I think the site does a pretty good job of reporting concise little bits of interesting financial news with opinions about how it might affect your investments.

Admittedly, I'm a tech junkie. I stood in line for 2 hours to buy the first iPhone when it came out, and I've upgraded every version ever since. I also love my iPad. **If you own a smart phone or an iPad, there are some great Financial Planning Apps for these devices**.

CashFlow - This is a free app that lets you manage all your expenses. Proper tracking and management of your income and expenses forms the basis of proper financial planning.

With CashFlow you can promptly record your daily cash receipts, expenses and even your ATM balances, thus making it possible to track historical cash flow information.

CashFlow also gives you the opportunity to adequately describe the nature of these transactions and export them in CSV and OFX format over a course of 30, 60 or 90 days as desired.

This app has an in-built calculator to help you track these cash flows and determine balances in a simple manner. For multi-national usage, Cash-Flow free for iPad is available in several languages including English, Japanese, Korean, Spanish and Russian among others.

Suffice it to say that with CashFlow you will not need to see your bank statement before being able to make reconciliations on a monthly basis. Also you will be able to effectively manage your finances and track how much you have spent in real time terms.

Bloomberg - To aid cash management and what exactly you spend your money on, you need to have the best and reliable financial information at your finger tips. Bloomberg for iPad is one great free financial apps that opens you to real time financial information globally.

According to some analysts, Bloomberg is the "most trusted source for financial information online and it's loaded with tools to help you analyze the world's markets in real time". With Bloomberg you get stock information across several markets, breaking financial news, industry information and trends etc.

Also, you can create a specific list of stocks and market you wish to follow on Bloomberg, including RSS feeds for specific financial news across the world.

Jumsoft Money - is another free financial management app. It meets accounting needs of home businesses, small businesses, individuals, associations, clubs, and more. This app also lets you set and manage budget, manage multiple accounts, and see all types of reports about your money.

Easy Books is about the best, and also free app that serves as a fully fledged financial accounting module. It is ideal for small businesses and independent consultants/service providers who need to generate financial reports in real time.

Easy Books is also a fully integrated double entry accounting package that lets you input an unlimited number of transactions, including adding several features from compatible apps as you need them. In a way, Easy Books can be described as a financial Enterprise Resource Planning application, meaning you have access to all financial reports regardless of location and time.

Easy Books makes it possible to keep track of all your accounts including receivables, purchases, sales, assets, depreciation etc. Major financial reports that can be spooled from this app include your profit and loss statement, trial balance, aged debt analysis, and cash flow statement among others.

The capabilities of Easy Books are almost limitless as you can add accounts and report heading, including transaction lines without effort.

MoneyDance is another free money management app. It lets you quickly enter your expenses while you are on the move. It easily syncs with desktop version of MoneyDance, so you can easily manage your finances on both iPad, as well as your PC.

MoneyDance uses strong encryption to ensure that your data is secure when you try to sync your transactions on your local wi-fi.

FREE OFFER!

You Can Schedule A **FREE** Consultation With Bryan Now and Take The Guided Discovery™ Tour By Calling **1-800-546-0123**

Bryan is offering you a **FREE** guide called, "The Critical Questions You Must Ask To Get Your Financial Life In Order"

You can obtain the guide online at:
http://www.VellumFinancial.com/freeguide

Made in the USA
San Bernardino, CA
29 March 2018